CYNTHIA HART'S VICTORIANA 1996 DIARY

WORKMAN PUBLISHING
NEW YORK

For my friend, Pat Upton

For his photographic expertise, dedication to excellence and his consistently sunny disposition I thank Steven Tex. For the loan of antique jewelry and silver objects, I thank Ilene Chazanof, Decorative Arts (New York City). For their generous loans of vintage Victorian garments, laces, dolls and other antique objects, I thank Kaethe and Jules Kliot, Lacis (Berkeley, CA), Yvonne Miller, The Dolls Corner (Scotch Plains, NJ), Kathy and Al Raymond, Starr Ockenga, Regina Sugrue and Virginia Makis. I thank Jean and Howard Berg for their support and encouragement. I also thank Sharyn Prentiss, Nancy Lindemeyer, Sally Kovalchick, Pat Upton, Carbery O'Brien, Gwen Goldman, Erica Ando, Harumi Ando and Thomas Ando-Hart for their enthusiasm and gracious help.

The photographic illustrations for this calendar were created by Cynthia Hart and recorded on film by Steven Tex. All of the antique paper ephemera not otherwise credited is from Cynthia Hart's Collection of Cherished Images.

Copyright © 1995 by Cynthia Hart. All rights reserved.

No portion of this publication may be reproduced—mechanically, electronically, or by any other means, including photocopying—without written permission of the publisher.

Published by
Workman Publishing Company, Inc.
708 Broadway
New York, NY 10003-9555

Printed in Hong Kong
ISBN: 0-7611-0008-3

Like a favorite friend,
may this little volume bring you
joy and comfort all year—
beginning to end.

Happy 1996!

Cynthia Hart

JANUARY

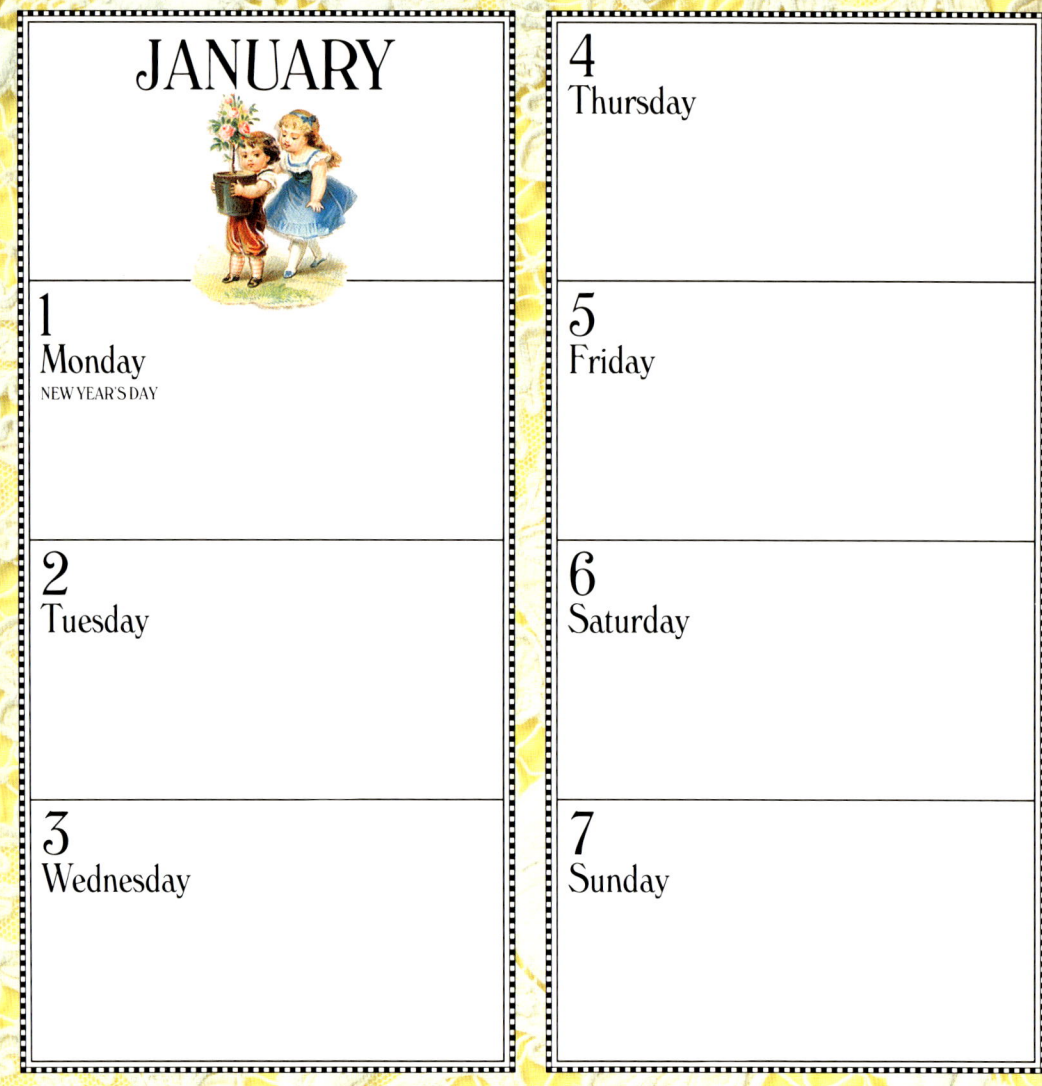

1
Monday
NEW YEAR'S DAY

2
Tuesday

3
Wednesday

4
Thursday

5
Friday

6
Saturday

7
Sunday

JANUARY

8
Monday

9
Tuesday

10
Wednesday

| 11 Thursday |
| 12 Friday |
| 13 Saturday |
| 14 Sunday |

JANUARY

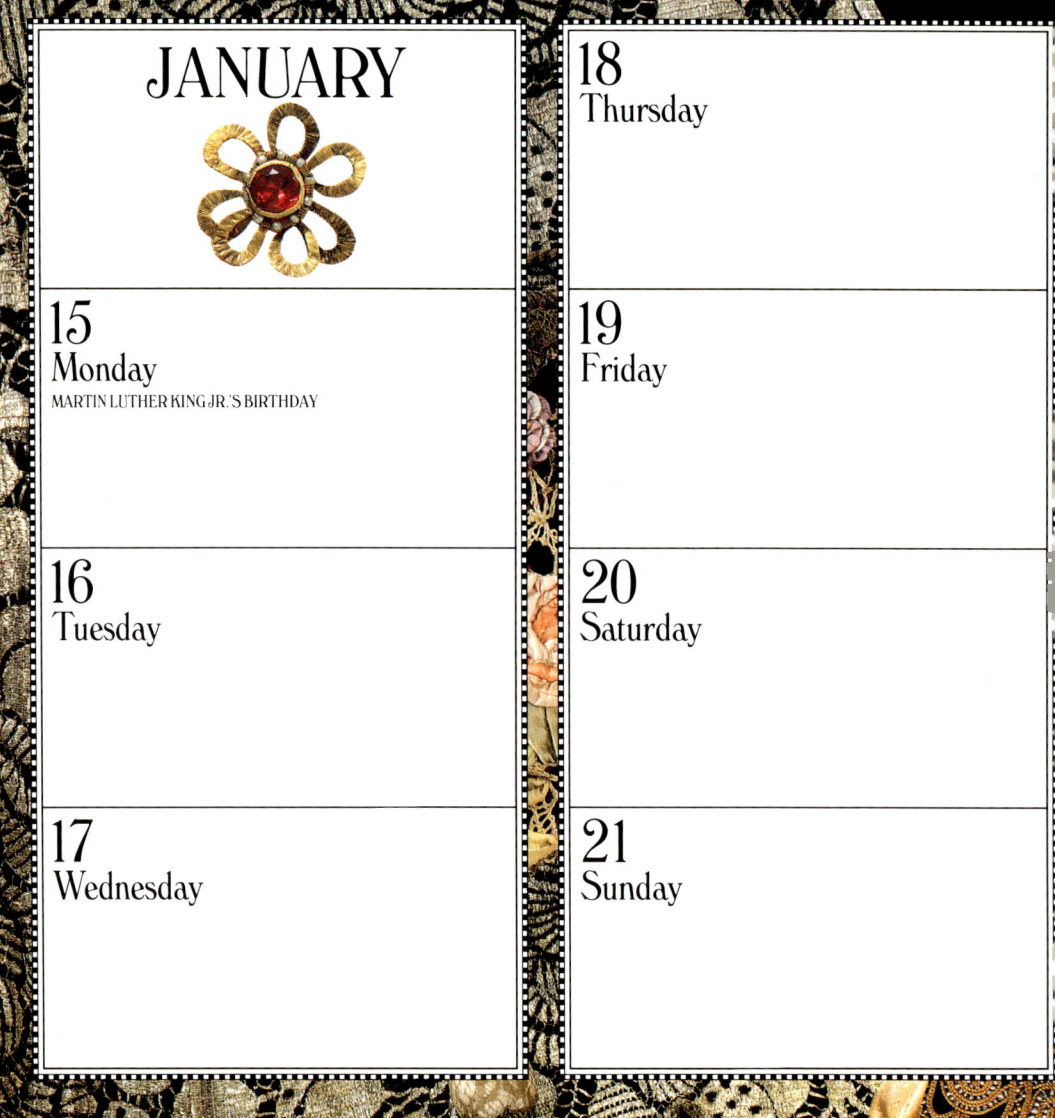

15 Monday
MARTIN LUTHER KING JR.'S BIRTHDAY

16 Tuesday

17 Wednesday

18 Thursday

19 Friday

20 Saturday

21 Sunday

JANUARY

22
Monday

23
Tuesday

24
Wednesday

25 Thursday

26 Friday

27 Saturday

28 Sunday

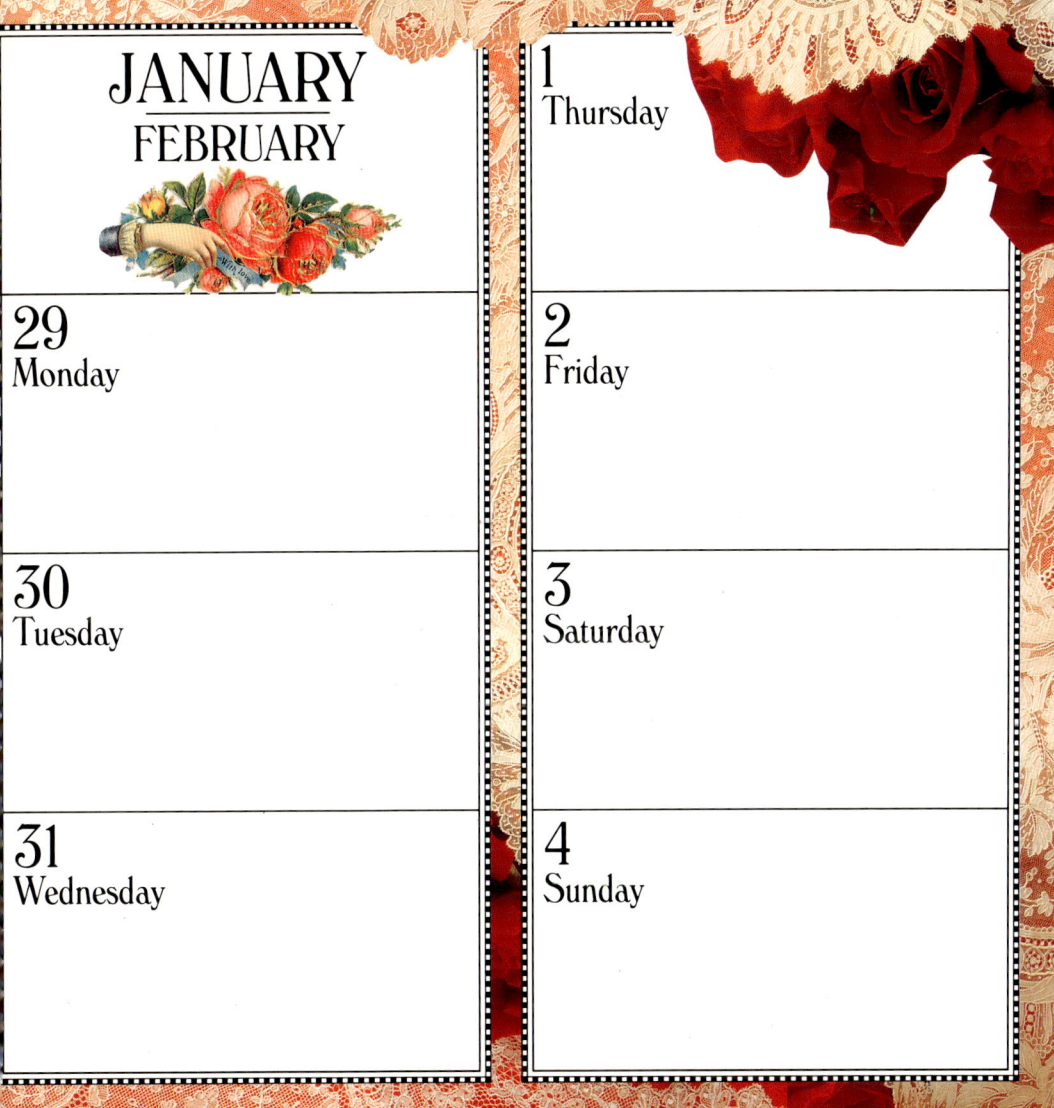

JANUARY
FEBRUARY

1 Thursday

29 Monday

2 Friday

30 Tuesday

3 Saturday

31 Wednesday

4 Sunday

FEBRUARY

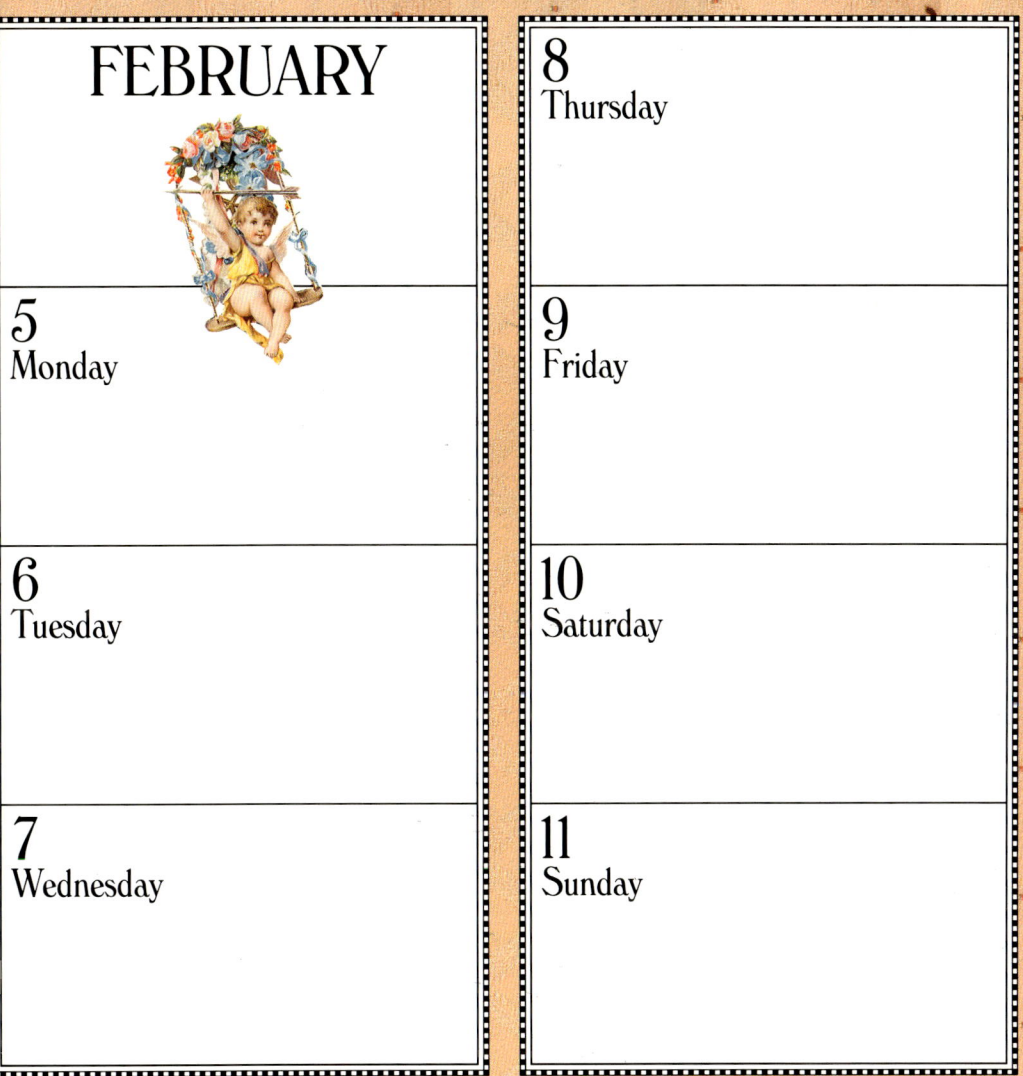

5
Monday

6
Tuesday

7
Wednesday

8
Thursday

9
Friday

10
Saturday

11
Sunday

FEBRUARY

12
Monday
LINCOLN'S BIRTHDAY

13
Tuesday

14
Wednesday
VALENTINE'S DAY

15 Thursday

16 Friday

17 Saturday

18 Sunday

FEBRUARY

19
Monday
PRESIDENTS DAY

20
Tuesday

21
Wednesday
ASH WEDNESDAY

22
Thursday
WASHINGTON'S BIRTHDAY

23
Friday

24
Saturday

25
Sunday

FEBRUARY
MARCH

26
Monday

27
Tuesday

28
Wednesday

29
Thursday

1
Friday

2
Saturday

3
Sunday

MARCH

4
Monday

5
Tuesday

6
Wednesday

7
Thursday

8
Friday

9
Saturday

10
Sunday

MARCH

11 Monday

12 Tuesday

13 Wednesday

14 Thursday

15 Friday

16 Saturday

17 Sunday
ST. PATRICK'S DAY

MARCH

18
Monday

19
Tuesday

20
Wednesday

21
Thursday

22
Friday

23
Saturday

24
Sunday

MARCH

25
Monday

26
Tuesday

27
Wednesday

28
Thursday

29
Friday

30
Saturday

31
Sunday
PALM SUNDAY

4
Thursday
PASSOVER

5
Friday
GOOD FRIDAY

6
Saturday

7
Sunday
EASTER

APRIL

8 Monday

9 Tuesday

10 Wednesday

11 Thursday

12 Friday

13 Saturday

14 Sunday

APRIL

15
Monday

16
Tuesday

17
Wednesday

18
Thursday

19
Friday

20
Saturday

21
Sunday

APRIL

22
Monday

23
Tuesday

24
Wednesday

25
Thursday

26
Friday

27
Saturday

28
Sunday

APRIL
MAY

29
Monday

30
Tuesday

1
Wednesday

2
Thursday

3
Friday

4
Saturday

5
Sunday

MAY

6 Monday

7 Tuesday

8 Wednesday

9
Thursday

10
Friday

11
Saturday

12
Sunday
MOTHER'S DAY

MAY

13
Monday

14
Tuesday

15
Wednesday

16
Thursday

17
Friday

18
Saturday

19
Sunday

MAY

20
Monday
VICTORIA DAY (CANADA)

21
Tuesday

22
Wednesday

23
Thursday

24
Friday

25
Saturday

26
Sunday

MAY
JUNE

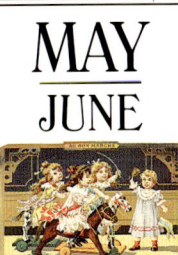

27
Monday
MEMORIAL DAY OBSERVED

28
Tuesday

29
Wednesday

30
Thursday
TRADITIONAL MEMORIAL DAY

31
Friday

1
Saturday

2
Sunday

JUNE

3
Monday

4
Tuesday

5
Wednesday

6
Thursday

7
Friday

8
Saturday

9
Sunday

JUNE

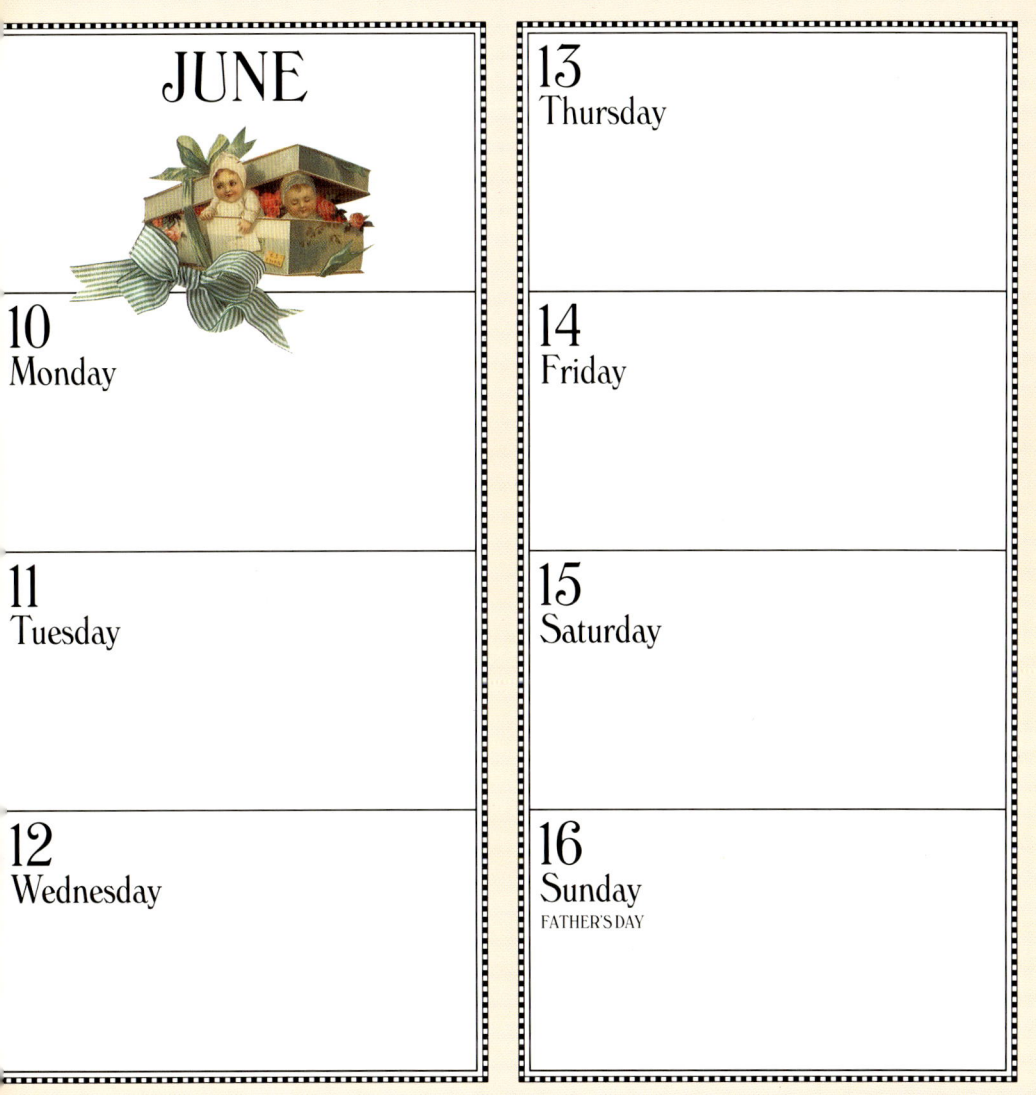

10
Monday

11
Tuesday

12
Wednesday

13
Thursday

14
Friday

15
Saturday

16
Sunday
FATHER'S DAY

JUNE

17
Monday

18
Tuesday

19
Wednesday

20
Thursday

21
Friday

22
Saturday

23
Sunday

JUNE

24
Monday
ST. JEAN BAPTISTE DAY (CANADA)

25
Tuesday

26
Wednesday

27
Thursday

28
Friday

29
Saturday

30
Sunday

JULY

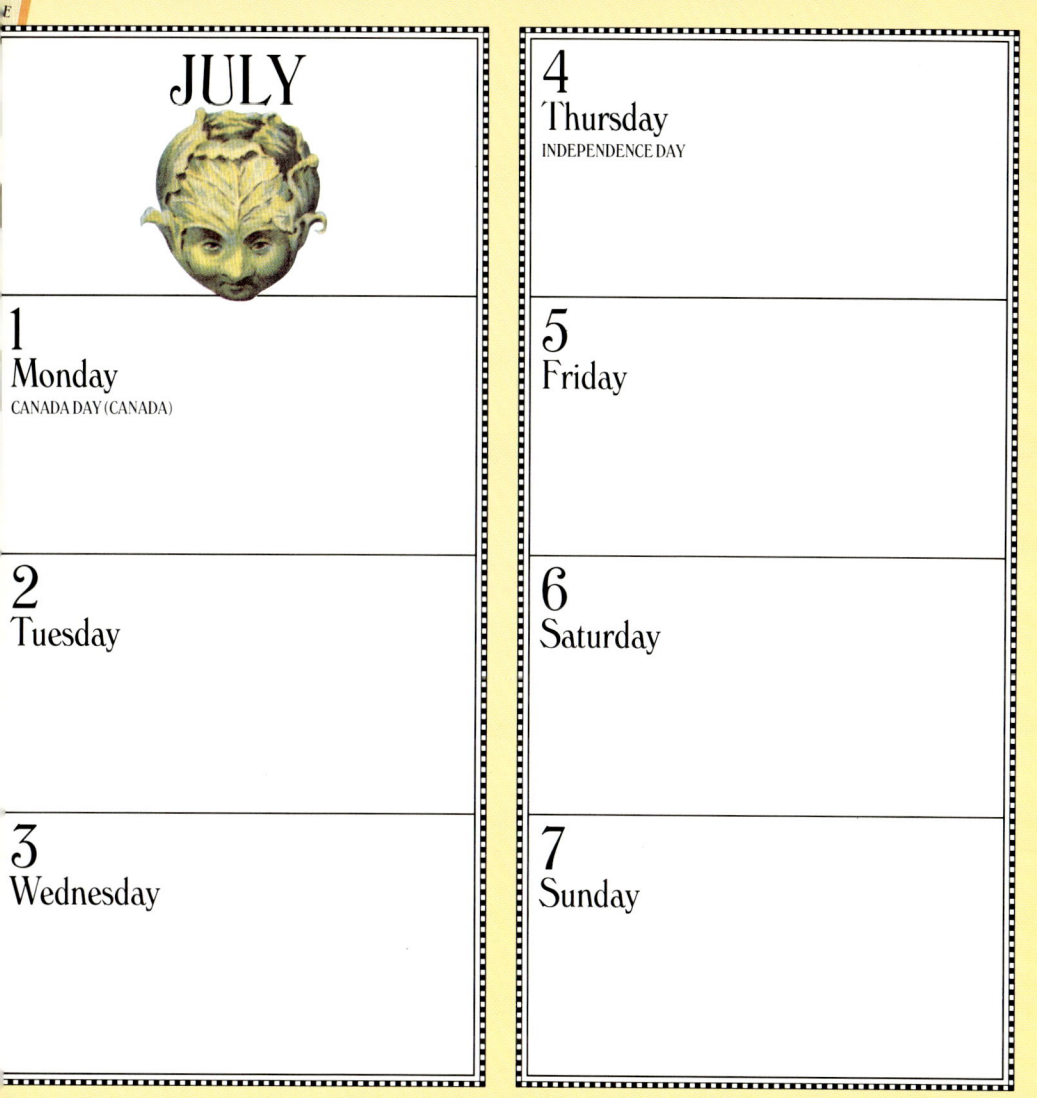

1
Monday
CANADA DAY (CANADA)

2
Tuesday

3
Wednesday

4
Thursday
INDEPENDENCE DAY

5
Friday

6
Saturday

7
Sunday

JULY

8
Monday

9
Tuesday

10
Wednesday

11
Thursday

12
Friday

13
Saturday

14
Sunday

JULY

15 Monday

16 Tuesday

17 Wednesday

18 Thursday

19 Friday

20 Saturday

21 Sunday

JULY

22
Monday

23
Tuesday

24
Wednesday

25
Thursday

26
Friday

27
Saturday

28
Sunday

JULY
AUGUST

29 Monday

30 Tuesday

31 Wednesday

1
Thursday

2
Friday

3
Saturday

4
Sunday

AUGUST

5
Monday
CIVIC HOLIDAY (CANADA)

6
Tuesday

7
Wednesday

8
Thursday

9
Friday

10
Saturday

11
Sunday

AUGUST

12 Monday

13 Tuesday

14 Wednesday

15 Thursday

16 Friday

17 Saturday

18 Sunday

AUGUST

19 Monday

20 Tuesday

21 Wednesday

22 Thursday

23 Friday

24 Saturday

25 Sunday

AUGUST
SEPTEMBER

26
Monday

27
Tuesday

28
Wednesday

29
Thursday

30
Friday

31
Saturday

1
Sunday

SEPTEMBER

2
Monday
LABOR DAY

3
Tuesday

4
Wednesday

5
Thursday

6
Friday

7
Saturday

8
Sunday
GRANDPARENTS DAY

SEPTEMBER

9
Monday

10
Tuesday

11
Wednesday

12
Thursday

13
Friday

14
Saturday
ROSH HASHANAH

15
Sunday

SEPTEMBER

16
Monday

17
Tuesday

18
Wednesday

19
Thursday

20
Friday

21
Saturday

22
Sunday

SEPTEMBER

23
Monday
YOM KIPPUR

24
Tuesday

25
Wednesday

26
Thursday

27
Friday

28
Saturday

29
Sunday

SEPTEMBER
OCTOBER

30 Monday

1 Tuesday

2 Wednesday

3 Thursday

4 Friday

5 Saturday

6 Sunday

OCTOBER

7
Monday

8
Tuesday

9
Wednesday

10
Thursday

11
Friday

12
Saturday
TRADITIONAL COLUMBUS DAY

13
Sunday

OCTOBER

14
Monday
COLUMBUS DAY OBSERVED
THANKSGIVING (CANADA)

15
Tuesday

16
Wednesday

17
Thursday

18
Friday

19
Saturday

20
Sunday

OCTOBER

21 Monday

22 Tuesday

23 Wednesday

24 Thursday

25 Friday

26 Saturday

27 Sunday

OCTOBER
NOVEMBER

28
Monday

29
Tuesday

30
Wednesday

31
Thursday
HALLOWEEN

1
Friday

2
Saturday

3
Sunday

NOVEMBER

4 Monday

5 Tuesday
ELECTION DAY

6 Wednesday

7 Thursday

8 Friday

9 Saturday

10 Sunday

NOVEMBER

11
Monday
VETERANS DAY
REMEMBRANCE DAY (CANADA)

12
Tuesday

13
Wednesday

14
Thursday

15
Friday

16
Saturday

17
Sunday

NOVEMBER

18 Monday

19 Tuesday

20 Wednesday

21 Thursday

22 Friday

23 Saturday

24 Sunday

NOVEMBER
DECEMBER

25 Monday

26 Tuesday

27 Wednesday

28
Thursday
THANKSGIVING

29
Friday

30
Saturday

1
Sunday

DECEMBER

2
Monday

3
Tuesday

4
Wednesday

5
Thursday

6
Friday
HANUKKAH

7
Saturday

8
Sunday

DECEMBER

9
Monday

10
Tuesday

11
Wednesday

12
Thursday

13
Friday

14
Saturday

15
Sunday

DECEMBER

16 Monday

17 Tuesday

18 Wednesday

19 Thursday

20 Friday

21 Saturday

22 Sunday

DECEMBER

23
Monday

24
Tuesday

25
Wednesday
CHRISTMAS

26
Thursday
BOXING DAY (CANADA)

27
Friday

28
Saturday

29
Sunday

DECEMBER
JANUARY

30
Monday

31
Tuesday

1
Wednesday
NEW YEAR'S DAY

2
Thursday

3
Friday

4
Saturday

5
Sunday

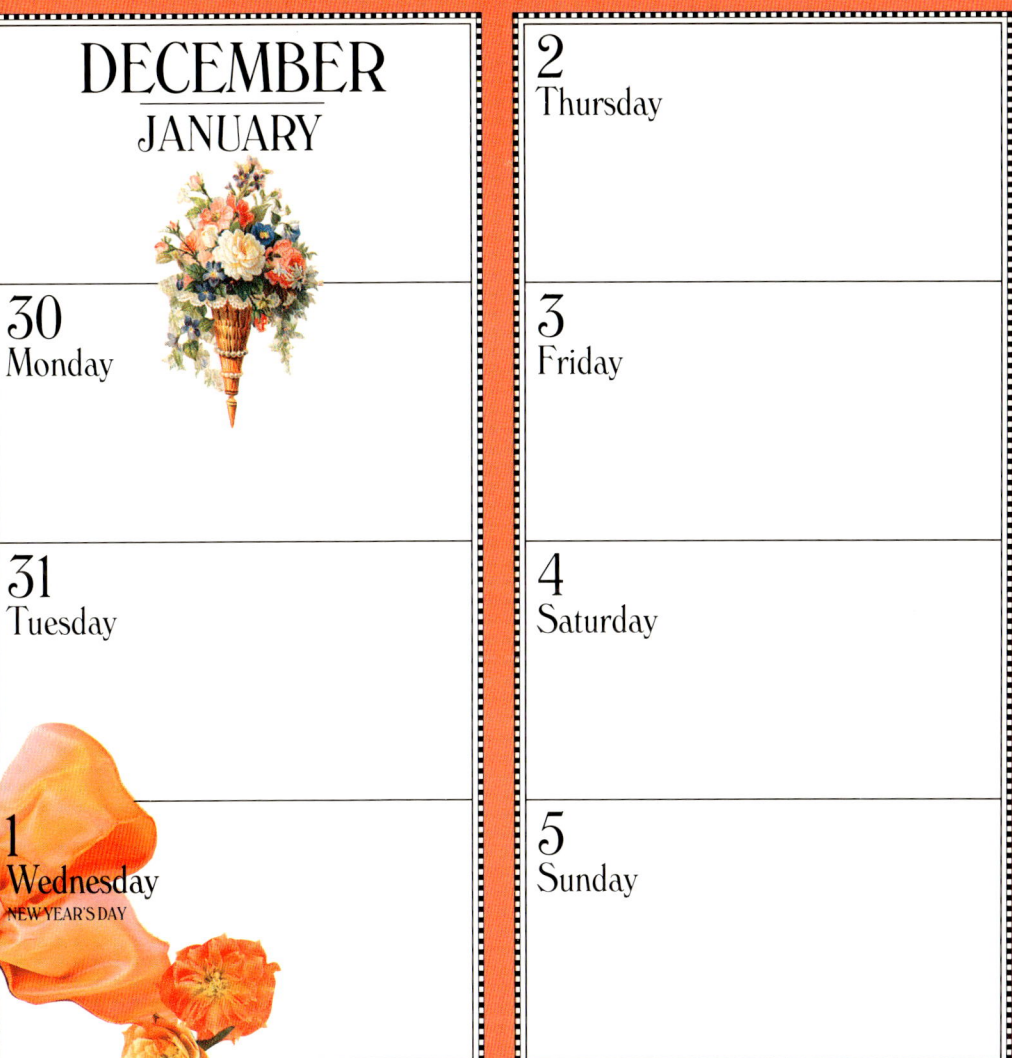

The antique paper items used in the collages for this calendar were printed in the last half of the nineteenth century or the very earliest years of the twentieth century using a now unused form of commercial printing called chromolithography.

NOTES

NOTES

NOTES

NOTES

NOTES

NOTES

NOTES

NOTES